T0380822

7 Ways To Empower WOMEN

STANDING LIKE A TREE

Dory Anne Louise

Balboa Press books may be ordered through booksellers or by contacting:

Balboa Press
A Division of Hay House
1663 Liberty Drive
Bloomington, IN 47403
www.balboapress.com
1 (877) 407-4847

Interior Image Credit: Dory Anne Louise

ISBN: 978-1-9822-3685-4 (sc)
ISBN: 978-1-9822-3686-1 (e)

Print information available on the last page.

Balboa Press rev. date: 10/21/2019

BALBOA.PRESS
A DIVISION OF HAY HOUSE

7 Ways to *Empower* WOMEN

STANDING LIKE A TREE

By Dory Anne Louise

My tree has many branches where I help others, and now it is time to share ways toward self-empowerment of all women who feel the need to grow stronger and more confident; claiming self-empowerment as one's right.

Contents

It is time...

Time to gather all women for a powerful and confident way of living life well

The many faces of strong women

By Dory Anne Louise

Dedication

This book is dedicated to everyone who feels as if they need a new perspective in life that includes their own point of view about meaningful accomplishments that bring about purpose in life's adventures and challenges. Both men and women can benefit from reading *7 Ways to Empower Women.* Men can begin to understand women better through standing by their woman's side in their growth and development. Women can reach for the sky with the many lessons on how to be stronger and self-empowered; bringing these concepts to their sons and daughters. Empowerment practice is for everyone who chooses creative confidence and strength building times in life that bring about stillness, calmness and balance. Claim your right to be strong and pass self-empowerment philosophy to others on your path in life.

Empower yourself

One person can change everything for many people, just as one flower is as uniquely guided by spirit and nature to grow and blossom

Our oneness with each other is our connection; feeling the pull of energy toward those who cross our paths happens in every moment. You can help many people by changing yourself to be more controlled with your present step in life's many challenges, and passing along knowledge related to confidence and strength to others who need a new direction filled with optimism that each moment can and will be a solid step to take toward self-empowering ways.

Introduction

I know many people who feel the way I do; finding happiness through others' perspective; holding close to the idea that it is a good thing to help others find their way.

What about you?

Are you older now and finding that people around you are leading their own lives happily but you are still struggling with the choices that you have made?

Are they really your own choices?

Some choices are not really your own doing; someone in your life may be pushing you in one direction or the other.

Can you remember the last time you did something that was truly your idea?

I have just begun to see that I do have many choices to lead myself toward but I continue to have trouble deciding where to begin. I begin with doing the one thing that I love the most, that is my artwork and writing where I lose myself in meaningful waves of positive energy that gives me an internal bliss, and I will continue on that path until it does not fit me.

What do you love to do the most?

You can be happier if you give into what your desires in life are. Even if it means you need to make some changes that may be painful; begin now. Begin now with your transformation by doing it with speed and agility or by doing it slow and persistent, but begin to do something that truly makes you feel happy inside so that your soul feels good and loving.

Do not wait too long to include yourself in a happy, new way about you

Your internal soul is waiting for you to make some decisions about life; begging you to choose yourself this time; including a dynamically fun and happy moment that will change your perspective on personal internal joyfulness and hopefulness about the rest of your life. Save some time for you right now, it may be just the thing to do in this moment. You have been the busy one; taking care of others all of your life, what about you?

Finding your strength

Life is like a tree, you grow stronger with your roots spreading to different areas of your timeline where passions are waiting for you to pick them up again; casting that last stone of wellness into deep waters, providing you with the ripple effect of oneness with yourself, nature and others. You are a tree, standing strong and centered today; reaching up for hope, not looking back, or too far ahead of yourself. Be strong and be flexible in your quest of unending wellness in mind, body and spirit. Take each piece of you; finding ways to move to a balance and center in each area of your being.

When I begin empowering myself, *mind adventures* come to me as I find a good book to read that encourages me to embrace hope in my next step in living my life well, and as my spirit rises above to clarify my direction down the path, I smile. When I want to be stronger in my physical being I push myself just a little more each day to do something that challenges my body such as a good yoga stretch or a long walk to engage myself in the surrounding places of nature.

What is it that you do to gain strength in your mind, body and soul? Take it back; that place you used to go to that brings you power. Has it been a long time since you felt *a powerful flow* of energy that pushes you with renewed momentum? You can bring that feeling back into your life.

Strong Women

I have been accused of being a warrior woman. I am a standing tall, strong person who gets through just about anything in life including horror and traumatic times that appear in what seems like a timeless vortex of spinning, dusty and dirty winds, but my warrior stance gets me through to a place of wellness.

The need for connection and oneness with others

Know that it may not be strength that holds us steadfast and planted like a tree in life; it is about those around who stand by and assist in the good and hard times. Those people we are connected to give us the strength to carry on. I know I will have both good and bad days but I adjust daily to the *weather* changes in my life.

I cannot predict my future or stay in the past where I cannot change anything. There is only one time, and that is this present moment. There will be days where many tears fall like raindrops on a stormy day; well -hidden tears of blue tinted salty waves that appear without a moment's notice; I am there, picking up the pieces of the puzzle I have to complete. I have great days of pleasure and insight into where I need to be in life that help me to grow stronger and wiser.

Today in this moment

Today I am the warrior; strong enough now to get through those hard days because many people helped me down the road of life, especially mom who appeared fragile at times but underneath was a warrior woman who took on everyone and everything that life brought to her.

Mom's strength remains with me; reminding me that a warrior can be built like a strong bridge that crosses over to the other side of life where the grass is green and the flowers are a perfect shade of violet. Now that mom is spirit, I feel her unending presence as if she is near, keeping a watchful, loving eye on me.

Imagine Inside where that strong person resides

No one really knows what I am thinking about inside of my soul but it may show a bit on my face in a frown or smile because I am not good at hiding things inside. We all have a place where we keep things hidden until we are ready to explore within, or express some inner thoughts and feelings with others.

Practice makes perfect is a good saying when it comes to happy things to do with life but if I visualize some sadness or unhappiness inside, I may need to talk about it because some things have not *settled down* in a good place for me and I may need to *adjust my sails* to balance my inner being emotionally and spiritually. What do you see when you imagine the spirit inside of yourself?

Things that keep me working on Self- Empowerment and letting go

I express my inner self through artistic endeavors that allow my soul to take over. I fix my inner puzzles in life with some color and design, and others thank me for being so self- revealing; teaching them how to flow through colorful times that allow for letting go of things in life that may stagnate progress toward creating passionate living.

Mistakes

It takes time, much practice and many mistakes with a paint brush to feel secure when *therapeutic waves of energy* pass through me. Painting brings out my inner soul to say *hello* to myself and others who may need some shades of blues, greens, yellows and pinks in their lives.

When is it your time to be expressive?

Is now the right time?

Are you finding yourself painting a picture, writing a song or visualizing a green meadow of love in meditation?

Are you practicing self-love in many phases of your mind, body and soul?

Do you want to grow stronger and wiser as you practice creative, self- empowering and confidence building challenges?

Strengthening my many different faces with internal self-love

Imagine Outside

How do people see you?

Does your outward appearance seem to be working well?

Do others believe that you are fine; a completely well-rounded individual who is making it through life in a meaningful, purposeful way, but you are not feeling very confident? At different stages of life we may go through times of grief and sadness that can be covered up quite well with a nice smile, grin; even laughter that conceals what is really inside, and we may do this very effectively for a long time.

How I have seen my outside in the past

In my past I worried about how people felt about me, and wanted them to think "I had it all together." My life was one happy time after another with me keeping score for myself on what I had or have not been doing in life that seemed on the outside inviting and challenging. Today, my outside is transparent, people know who I am; the good and bad things about me are visible to all who know me. This has been a change I have been working on for a long time that is very self-empowering; allowing others to know who I really am.

Positive Affirmations on Self-Empowerment

Through my internal, spiritual self I feel strength today as if I am a strong tree, centered and balanced. No one can compare to my spiritual strength, my mind power or my physical being. I grow each day to the quiet sounds of my roots pushing into the ground and my arms stretching to the sky.

I am noticing everything today

I see details in a pink flower struggling to stand strong against an unending windy day. I see the softness of tiny lines in a face I know so well, as I focus on the smile lines that look so nice. I find I can embrace the different shades of green in my mind and soul with grass that covers my toes as I walk barefoot through time; finding myself singing a melody soothing to my soul, even when I am not in tune.

Daughters

My daughters call me *Warrior Woman* as they speak openly to me with deep sincerity, "You came through the tunnel of life with many scratches and bruises and a broken heart, but you stayed who you are throughout the struggle. You are definitely a Warrior, stronger than anyone we know." Both women and men need to know that life continues to be a struggle with many chances and decisions to make. At times you make the right choice in life, and sometimes you do not. The failures become lessons on how to empower yourself in mind, body and spirit.

See your many choices with clarity that floats in the blue stream of life. The flowers of life are all beautiful with purple waves of life adventures; some linger in their beauty and some pass along as lessons on how life unfolds; filled with good and not so good happenings.

Focus on yourself. Love every part of your being.

In order to be empowered, one must focus first on liking and then loving oneself. The love of **you** is the first lesson on empowerment. The floating lily stays strong, floating in water, untouched by the forces of nature. You too are a lily floating on top of life and its adventures when you begin a journey that includes self-love and love for others.

The warrior woman

She stands strong and centered, balancing herself on one foot. That is what internal power is, powerful balancing, and knowing that you need balance in life through many practice hours; helping with strengthening and flexibility in mind, body and soul.

Yoga is finding my personal stillness in mind, body and soul. When I practice yoga I can find spaces of light in those tiny cracks I see in alone time with breath work; standing tall as if I am truly a dancer where I have to push against the earth as I stand strong, reaching for the sky. *Dancer* pose is a sturdy one that is full of strength, self- empowerment and balance.

Yoga becomes my *inside* self as the spirit and mind merge in calmness and stillness of the pose I stay in to release all that is not calm or not centered. I become part of the dancer as I stand on the edge of time with a challenge of a one legged standing pose. Dancer is where you may need to be to embrace the concept of a new you who is self-confident with strong self- esteem. You are one within the merge of mind, body and spirit.

Dancer Pose in the strength of a warrior woman

Focus on your balance. Where are you right now in your personal center of life? Are you standing strong, or on the edge of a cliff?

A single flower has many parts as you do. Look closely and see the petals of just one flower. That is where you need to be; focused on the beauty inside and outside of yourself; only then will you see the many details you possess.

1.

Find your completed self

Can you envision this? This completed painting like you evolves and changes into what you need and want in life. Can you start something new to help you gain the self-confidence you desire?

You are thriving to become empowered; a completed self, from black and white to the fullness of color (Entitled: *Swaying trees in the Breezes of Summer*)

Plant the seeds of empowerment, water it well and reap beautiful flowers

To change something about myself I must change my perspective, and then I can add some new and challenging adventures such as new hobbies I want to develop into reality. I can fail at new things but at times I succeed. Change has a yin and yang effect. Up and down I go, knowing at all times, giving up is not an option.

Changes and expansion

I remember as a child I did not think I could do many things. My physical being was in need of change, some which could be fixed, like flat feet, chubby being, and other things like low self- esteem needed a lot of work but I never gave up. I excelled at things that fit my physicality such as yoga, walking and riding a bike. That is the first step to self-empowerment, finding places and things to do for betterment that are a good fit for you.

What is it that you are excellent at? You must have something that drives you as you move about down the timeline of life where there are many choices to make, and changes to complete in order to be the best you can be. Take some chances and experiment with new adventures in life that are a good fit for your being. Self-improvement of your mind, body and spirit can be good first steps toward a healthy lifestyle.

The Outside

On the outside everyone sees who I am. I exist as a being with flaws, and perhaps bits of nice parts like a pretty face, smile or long legs, but that is the outside; my body. Inside of my spirit I have insight into myself in places that calm my internal soul where soft music is playing as I dance to my own tune.

In dreams there are beautiful visions that take me to different places of my life. I love the sandy beach times where everything is still as I stop time and see myself endlessly walking and collecting soft edged blue and green glass. I feel the edges of the glass for a moment to make sure it has no sharpness, and place it into my pocket with care. I am about 10 years old, exploring unusual things near Lake Erie beach where there are many pleasurable moments as I look down the rocky, brown and gray sandy beach to a lighthouse in the distance that is behind soft white clouds, as I say to myself, "Someday

I will make it to the lighthouse to climb to the top to see the endless, blue lake full of the sounds of crashing white waves of wonder." My spirit lifts me up to see the lake in its splendor, and as I peer into the dusty, dirty windows of the lighthouse, I become even more passionate about being near water and its powerful waves. I know that I too can become powerful like water; flowing softly or crashing loudly against life and its many challenges.

How are your inner and outer places in life?

Beginnings can be traumatic and may not work out the way you want them to.

The beginning of this painting entitled: *Swaying trees in the breezes of summer* was a struggle for me until completion. I almost gave up on painting this.

Can you complete the picture of your life into a beautiful painting full of blues, yellows and greens; turning the black and white wave that embraces you right now into a colorful and stronger moment from this day forward?

Begin a Disappearing act that brings on peace as mindfulness grows

Things go by in flashes or slowly like a blue stream that I wade through in my journey through life. Everything disappears and past moments are good to linger on but forward is better with present creative times unending as I cruise through soft times with soft breezes touching my hair as it moves slowly with my mind and body like a romantic song. I am rocking to the tune as if dancing quietly inside as I disappear into another dream.

Thriving is more...

Doing more than surviving the many moments in life is the way to many passionate and creative challenges that include self-improvement and confidence building. Small improvements become motivation that I need to take me to self- efficacy, and that first positive step of a new beginning. I remember thriving in a world where I was doing things that I enjoyed. My most thriving moments are when I am lost in my artistic endeavors; climbing out of the dullness of work into the massive exploration of a creative, artistic moment. I remember my struggle as a young adult where I did have many failures before success in life. I never gave up on my dreams although realities got in the way at times with juggling child rearing and my own personal needs. Through all the ups and downs, I knew that staying in a positive perspective would help me to become a thriving adult.

Natural happenings

You can begin your journey through nature and its beauty. This will bring you closer to your many selves, especially spirit which will bring you closer to self-empowerment. When you are surrounded by nature in a peaceful state of mind where all things have clarity like a blue stream is flowing through you in a calmness that brings you an energizing bliss; that is when you will find your personal wonder.

My Bliss

Trees sprinkle their dewy ways as I walk today at first believing it was still raining but then realizing that the trees were shaking their lovely green leaves, leaving me with the warmth of a summer shower as the birds danced in wonder, bouncing up and down. I believe nature is an opening to each day where I can shake off negative feelings in the sprinkling, dewy mornings as I walk in silence.

It is time to empower

Dare I take any credit for accomplishments and challenges I have taken in life?

These are the words of many women who feel that their lives have not been full of empowering times that could have made things better and helped with growth and strength.

Are things better today for women willing to take chances on themselves in the work world, at home accomplishments with raising children, writers and artist who have never evolved because of their gender into the creative whole being they should have been credited for?

Now is the time to reach deep into your soul and come out into the open. In your wonder years, whatever your age, you can dare to be an accomplished, wonder woman.

The opening of your door

Open your door today to something special. It does not have to be a large change. Can you do something that you know will make you feel different and whole? Continuing wellness depends upon touching every side of your many selves. This momentum that you create will propel you on toward even greater tasks that will make you feel like the door is opening to your future.

Touch your soul today with some wondrous feelings of being inside of yourself; places in your heart that need some attention. Create something that you can look at with a sense of accomplishment; making your creation colorful in blues, greens, yellows and reds.

Sit, stay still for a moment and remember those things in life that you have created. Those times when you walked through a great forest, looking up to the giant and strong trees that touched the sky. Their *wonder colors* of bright greens, oranges and yellows sparkle in your eyes at this moment. Remember when you helped someone who needed a friend to talk to, and you were busy but took the time to sit and listen to their troubles.

Loss

I remember a time when someone was leaving me and I had to keep a stiff upper lip as I felt tears streaming down like a faucet I could not shut off. This emotional side of me was my open door to helping others see that it is good to cry.

Begin to give yourself credit for all those that you have helped down this road of life. Be grateful that you are here today to be a friend to someone in need.

Begin again

In my beginning places, this is where I am; in the midst of fantasy or stark reality where everything is in its place except me. I walk around this fantasy world where no one else resides and make decisions about where I would like to be.

Wherever I am, I begin again, seeing things in drab grayness or in the light of day. I decide that today is a beautiful, sunny day full of orange rays. When I awaken, I begin again in a different perspective, fitting everything into places that complete my puzzle; knowing that many puzzles come with missing pieces.

2.

Never give up

I have to admit that many fears have surrounded me the past few years; finding ways to hide how I really felt about the changes, and not knowing which way to go. When I finally figured out that it really did not matter which way I went, I began to take some first steps in some challenging ways, knowing that life is like a circle; traveling first steps over and over again. I am happier now that I have released my fears and concerns to the universe; not feeling trapped by insecurities as I was in the past; embracing the present moment in prayer, silence and deep, cleansing breaths.

If you are waiting for something to change for you, the changes may not happen without assistance. You may need to make some plans on what you are going to do that will bring back passionate ways that give you momentum to never give up.

Passing along

You may pass along this way again where you find peace in familiar ways from the past that helped you to feel comfortable and grateful or you may move on to places in your heart that you have never visited before, and the view becomes amazing as you take one step closer to unknown places.

As life passes on like a steady drum beat, be the drummer making your life steady, strong and balanced.

Making needed changes

It is difficult to make changes in life at different junctures because you do not know for sure where you are going, especially in youth. Knowing that you have to do something with your life is the first step at any age.

I walk the beach looking at the changes in nature. The trees age as their roots spread deep and wide. The blue water of the lake nearby is not always blue and clear; changing to muddy waters as the snowy weather and wind direct it to stir up large waves that crash on the break wall of life.

Many people slow down when feeling challenged too much instead of pushing ahead in stagnating times. It may be time to think about where you are right now, and regroup on where you want to be.

Are you at the first step on a new journey or are you deep into something you have a great passion to complete?

Every day of my life I reassess where I am, and *adjust my sails*. I look deeply at all happenings in my life and find that they as lessons I can take with me to the next level of progress toward my goal. I plan, write things down as goals with objectives that I cross out daily. I implant in my heart the focus that everything comes from self- love and love for others. Love is a miracle to be valued and treasured. Learn from mistakes made on your path but do not dwell too long, do not repeat the same road, find new paths that feel right. Stay focused on the present moment; enjoying the loving, peaceful times.

Begin now and stop any procrastination

Making changes in life is a matter of steps; *baby steps* that take much thought and creative moments that guide me toward some trial and error challenges. I may be fearful of the newness of goals that seem to take a long time but I must remember to be patient with quests toward a new, more confident self.

Healthy Living is making the lifestyle changes that you need in order to stay well in mind, body and soul. There are many ingredients needed in a healthy living adventure including alternative modalities that center and balance the body; eating better and exercising more effectively. If you are just beginning, here are a few components that you may want to include:

Resiliency

A necessary component of self-empowerment is stamina; never giving up along the journey with continuing self-motivation that takes you to the next level of completing your goals.

An Optimistic view of life

When you practice being positive you develop the skill of self- confidence and self-empowerment. With practice you can create a personal script on being positive about your goals in life. Ask yourself, "How can I develop a more positive attitude?

Momentum

You need the ability to understand momentum. You become a rolling rock down a steep mountain that *propels* you into a spiral of healthy living activities that keep going and going!

Alternative modalities

Find a modality such as yoga, meditation, or tai chi that passively creates a slow and calm inner self; allowing you to get through the difficult times in life.

Healthy Readings

Prose and poetry can bring you to a more positive and optimistic wave of softness. You can read literature that inspires you or develop your own *flow words* that can calm your inner soul.

Calmness

Find ways to stay calm, centered and balanced in your mind, body and soul Calmness and balance are necessary components in a healthy living goal. Deep breathing exercises can slow breath and ease your mind.

Special Friends

Enlist others in the quest toward a healthy, self-confident goal. When you help others, you are helping yourself. Collaboration in a group effort creates a challenge and an ongoing connection that allows that extra push needed to get through the door of self-empowerment.

Self-efficacy

Find your personal self-efficacy and take the first step toward a healthier, balanced and centered person who has the internal motivation and momentum to begin a new dream with passion.

3.
Stay Self-Empowered

The Strength of a Dragon

The hero of this story is you

Every fairy tale has a hero who slays the dragon; strengthening their hero stance through fighting for a cause. The hero fights for the love they received from others, and needs to *pay it back*. In fairy tales, the hero faces their greatest challenge in life; finally attaining what they have strived for in life.

1. Take good care of yourself; finding internal pleasures that allows happiness and joy to grow in your mind, body and soul.
2. Make a list of your passions in life that you have been putting off and persist on developing what you need to be content in life.
3. Find ways to help others. This ingredient helps because when you help someone else you help yourself move toward happiness.
4. Know deep inside your *heart center* that you may need to change your attitude about happiness; realizing that you are the only one with the key to staying positive, hopeful and happy.
5. Become a thankful person. Thankful people are happy to just be here, in this present moment, taking their next breath.
6. Be accepting. Accept whatever it is that comes along in life; whether it is good or bad, it just is. Happiness comes with accepting what you cannot change.
7. Always be willing to change the things about yourself that others may notice are flaws. We all have them, and if someone is telling you that you need an *overhaul*, you probably do.
8. Take things in life slow and easy. Happy people do not rush; rushing brings on a stressful you! You need to *stop and smell the roses* very deeply so that you can wake up your happy senses. Surround yourself with color; sweet honeysuckle smells and sunshine to bring about a happy mood.
9. Above all, happy people know that they have to work on happiness and joy every single day; keeping it strong.
10. A good start to a joyful moment is putting a smile on your face with shoulders back, and head straight. A strong looking person becomes stronger through practicing *tree-like strength* that moves you toward a happy and content moment in time.

Remember that miracles do happen in life

When you are patient in life's events, miracles can happen. Remember that you may be someone's miracle right now; the person that has helped someone grow stronger and more confident.

Miracles

Miracles are spontaneous happenings that no one expects but they do happen. Even in the worse circumstances, thing can change; getting better because there is balance in the universe. Spiritual happenings are unfolding in miraculous ways.

The hope factor

Being hopeful and staying positive in bad situations can really help in life. There is much power in prayer and meditative ways. Healing occurs when you let go and just be. You can arouse your own positive energy from deep inside your inner core; awaiting the wisdom to let things unfold. You can hope for success, hope for acceptance, or hope that you can just hang on long enough to pass through to the other side of a life circumstance that may be a good situation right now.

Life has a yin and yang effect that balances the good and bad happenings. Everything in life miraculously gets better, and this becomes the miracle that you have been waiting for.

Practicing Patience

One of the most difficult things in my life is being patient with myself and others. I admit that I try to rush in, figure out what to do, and then move on quickly to another moment of *putting out a fire!*

Today, my goal is to stop and think about how important patience, stillness and calmness are to my health in mind body and spirit. As I speak these words, I promise my inner self that I will practice patience.

4.
On becoming a woman

As a child I did not know what empowerment meant to a woman's life. I felt as if I did not have much self-confidence or self-esteem; something I wanted desperately. I was meek and felt that I would always be misunderstood and not listened to.

I fell short of the mark in life; staying in safe places where self-empowerment would never be in my view. Self-confidence was only in tiny crack of light when I was seeking spirituality and oneness with myself. Empowerment was reserved for the strong-willed, not me.

During my entire life I tried to build my self- esteem through inner strength activities that people could see. I put myself and my creativity out there in the view of the public where I felt vulnerable. Why should anyone like my cartoons, my writings or any of my paintings, I am not sure about my talent?

Public speaking events were a challenge at first but eventually I was comfortable most of the time. When I finally became a self-empowered woman I did not know it. I still thought I needed much work and practice at being self-confident. When I looked into the mirror of life, I thought I was the same timid person, but I was not, I was strong and centered.

Today I go where I want to go. If I want to write a new book, I write it. If I want softness added to my being, I practice yoga, and if I want a challenging new experience I create it through my art. All of these creative and challenging experiences are a chance I take, knowing that they may not work out, and that is a good thing because life becomes even more empowering when there is some fear of failure. Today, I say to myself, "If I fail at this next project, it can help me learn about success."

I am a woman of power

Today people see me as a warrior with strength and balance in every step I take in life. As I grow older I realize how truly empowered I am and hope I can bring that feeling of "bring it on world," because I am ready and stronger than I ever thought was possible.

The most powerful woman I know is Angeline, my mother

The strongest woman I know can help everyone to discover secrets of self-esteem. Some thought Angel was weak, but she stood strong against all adversity; taking care of her children no matter what came into her life.

Angel took it all; the bad stuff with a smile and chuckle and the good with thankfulness and gratitude. She had a way about her that took years of practicing the skill of endurance. She was an athlete in mind and spiritual awakenings and is still with me as a guide in personal wellness that I dive into daily; starting my day with a walk; slow with purposeful, internal passionate thoughts or a fast pace to help my breath slow down and arise again like the bright yellow and orange sunny days that bring me not only comfort but motivation toward a life of peace. I remember Angel telling me her thoughts on relationships as I lie on her couch listening to music, she said, "Stay with your direction in life, even if it is difficult; becoming stronger each day. Never give up on yourself and your ability to help your children on their path toward self-empowerment, a strength that needs tending daily." Today I honor each day with a slow, deep breath of life where self-motivation becomes my mantra for personal endurance; keeping me sound, balanced and full of enough stamina to make my life a strong place to be. This enduring way is not without pain but is full of powerful waves of energy that grow inside of me each day.

Optimistic views

I try my best to stay in an optimistic flow; allowing any negative thoughts to enter my being but moving it quickly through my heart center; giving me continuing insight that tells me to move on and embrace only the good and challenging times that bring me love, passion and self-empowerment.

Chaotic Flowers; still and beautiful can show you a world where messy things can evolve into beautiful moments in life.

No regrets…

I clarify my next move in life like the game of Chess; strategic moves that are practiced and calculated with no regrets. I am a strong, empowered person who carries thoughts on success with me through all adventures. When success is not possible I know I have done my best.

Do people I know feel I take too many chances in life?

It does not matter what others think and do. I know that there are challenges I need to take that make my life a better place to be. I have no regrets; even the not so good happenings have given me a lesson. I move on in life, the past at my back and the future is unclear, but the now is good and solid. I will take chances that feel right and sturdy to me because what else is there besides taking a different look, a new perspective? Today I am in a place where I can walk around with a smile.

I accept changes in myself as I age, I have no other choice. I know that staying on the positive side of life is the place to be. I do not feel any older now, even though the pages of my life continue to unravel quickly like sand running through my fingers.

Taking some chances before my sand runs out

I know that it may seem like a wild idea; thoughts of challenges I need to take in order to become an official *Wild Woman*, who takes on the world with a loud thump. It is a good thing to have fears related to understanding myself and proceeding with my plans that will make me stronger. I will continue to find ways that support my efforts at growing stronger each and every day. What can you do to add strength to your life?

Practical Ways to become more empowered (Positive Affirmations)

1. I know that I am a powerful woman beyond belief. I do not focus on fear; I make my way toward the unknown with a strong desire on what I can do to help myself grow.
2. I can live life as a centered being that people honor and love.
3. I can begin new projects; creative ideas flow from me with effortless ease as I move toward completion. I always begin with a strong idea that has a beginning, middle and ending.

4. My objectives are clear. I am planning an extraordinary and powerful me.
5. I am thinking in a positive and optimistic way that allows for greatness to evolve in my life.
6. I generate ideas with others and together we plan well thought out creative idea that we complete.

Do something that helps others

At times I get lost in the possibilities of how to expand myself in mind, body and soul. When I remember what my goal in life is, it always comes back to how much I want to help others with their personal strength.

It is true that when I help others, I also help myself. In the past, I believed that it was the distraction of helping others with their confidence and empowerment that gave me some of my own passions and drives. What evolved in my own life was powerful strength and personal empowering ways propelled toward me like a blast of energy because I helped another person with their goals. What you give to others you get back in many ways.

Giving back

I remember working on a team building project as a nurse. I developed an entire program to share with my staff. My team building project consisted of visuals, handouts, physical examples such as role playing of the way we needed to get things done in the worksite. I was proud of how much I helped others collaborate; first learning how to work with each other, and then passing their knowledge to the patients at the psychiatric center who needed help with their mental illness. We had many creative times developing different programs for our patients that helped them grow stronger and become mentally and spiritually healthier.

Creative moments

What does it take to bring on a truly creative and empowering moment?

1. Many trial and error experiences
2. Joining together with others for collaboration on ideas that begin to work in a powerful way.

3. Never giving up on projects and new ideas.
4. Believing in yourself and your ability to take the first step toward your passions.

I believe that in order to grow into powerful women we have to embrace and help other woman. Together we can take on challenges and chances hard to go alone. We are a strong force; strengthening ourselves first and then moving it along to our daughters who need more power and self-confidence. Connection with other women creates a balance where we learn the shared lessons of fighting for rights we are entitled to have. Today, help someone; reach out and bring your confident self to another person; passing it along with love and wisdom to those who need your support. The world is changing and with the change brings more opportunities for women.

I was in leadership work most of my career as a nurse. I was strong but not strong enough to rise to the occasion of each difficulty I had as a supervisor. I backed down to the majority who were men, and even refused to be promoted a few times because I thought it would be too much for my emotional self. I felt as if I had too many feelings and emotions that would not be attended to if I took a large step toward *a men's world.*

Become a force in the world

Do not stop practicing self-empowering ways. At times it may seem easier to revert to the familiar, female self you were brought up to be; strong enough to go through childbirth and raise children but weak in other areas of your life such as the workplace. Remember who you are now and teach your children to become stronger and well balanced in life because of your example as a *Warrior Woman* full of power and enduring traits.

Bring hope and guidance to others

You are a *Warrior Woman* in your own right. Bring hope and guidance to women who may be struggling with inequalities and lack of change in the world where only men are counted on to lead others.

Competing

When I was a child I thought that I could compete in life with boys. As I grew up I was disappointed in being a girl. Girls were supposed to be thinking of marriage and rearing children. While I felt that it was important to have a family and children, I still wanted more in life such as a good job and enough money to get by. In the middle years from my thirties to fifties I did accomplish much on my own; making money that I saved from investment and savings, and allowing me to pay in part for my children's education.

Most of my life I had a partner so it was easier to stay in the *middle class road*. In between divorces I was poor. Therefore, early in life and at many junctures I had to fend for myself alone. When my youngest was fifteen I had to raise her on my own because of divorce. It was a difficult time in my life. I believe that women need to connect with other helpful women to share their stories on both good and bad times in life because sharing is the first step toward preparing oneself for the future and learning from each other.

Inside each circle is part of your life. You have many avenues to take, some will be good places and others will become your lessons on life that will take you toward your mission.

My mission in life is to help others to become successful

When you help others with your passionate ways, you help yourself. Passions and missions are the same for me. I am dedicated to bringing power to myself and others through my words where I bring light and clarity on ways to be sound in mind, body and soul.

Colorful times

People in my life have brought me here; places of colorful blues and yellows where everything is chaotic at first but then the colors blend together to create a spiritual place for me to be sound and balanced. I pick the color blue for quiet times and yellow for a glow I need at low times that changes into better feelings of hope and self-understanding because I have to understand myself before I can bring that understanding to you.

Does it matter that some things have to be in a chaotic way before the puzzle pieces connect?

Are you ready to begin a journey that may bring you both yin and yang times of pleasure and displeasure, because you have to experience both?

Can you enjoy your life taking many challenges that may or may not work out because you need success and failure to get through the closed doors of life?

My person

I do not have much to say about my childhood; it is unclear early on where I rode my bicycle barefoot in the summertime, and beach walked daily for colored glass and oddly shaped rocks. I can still see my coal colored feet, blackened by lack of shoes as mom stood by the doorway telling me, "Will you please put shoes on when you come into our home because you track dirt and whatever is on your feet into the living room where there is white carpeting." Mom was kind most of the time, never giving too much advice, but listening carefully to my daily rants about life and how hard it was.

Trauma in life

I believe I had some trauma in life that may have changed my perspective about trusting others.

The event I remember most clearly as a child was an older, small man dressed in a plaid blue and white shirt with gray, dirt colored whiskers on his chin walking through the tunnel near the beach. He reached out and grabbed one of my breasts as I walked through to the other side. I was 15 years old, with my sister, and when she saw what that man did, she ran, and as I chased after her I made her swear to never tell another soul about how that person assaulted me because dad would never let me walk outside alone again if he found out. Dad was very protective of his daughters to the point of trying his best to watch us closely. It did not work because we had many secret places that he could not find us. To dad's credit, I do believe that he did and still does love all three of his daughters very much. Trauma changes your life. It makes you feel untrusting of people and their intentions. Becoming more self-empowered and confident helps to bring back your trusting abilities and strengthens your core. Never let anyone take advantage of you. You deserve respect, kindness and trusting people in your life.

In youth everything appears in black and white. Color comes later where I can change things to whatever color I desire. Today I choose red flowers for growth and development of my warrior- self.

Reds wake up my soul

Adult life

Adulthood came quickly for me because I became a child bride at 18 years. I cried a lot but accepted the fact that I would be married and start a family. I was smart enough to know that it was too soon to have a child but I was able and willing to get through any door in life I encountered.

I believe that even as a child I was a strong *Warrior Woman* who accepted what was set before her. My career for most of my adult life was as a psychiatric nurse. Helping the mentally ill was a difficult task where there was danger everywhere but I wanted to assist people who were less fortunate than I was. I knew then that I had many skills in art, music, and writing that would help people who needed therapeutic interventions to bring them to a sound mind and spirit. We wore alarms around our necks that we could sound off if someone was acting dangerously.

I have seen men in a different light because of being taken advantage of early on. I felt that most men I knew tried to control me in many ways. It went to therapy through the years and grew stronger, finally becoming the person I want to be, in my own world where I am balanced, centered and self-empowered in life.

5.
Take time for spirit

Empowerment would not be a completed process without bringing spirituality into the arena for clarity and insight into how to be a happier person who is filled with joy and gratitude about life and the many adventures there are to take down the road of passions and creative awe moments where you cannot believe what is in front of you.

My passion in life has been to find places of oneness where I can go inside myself and share spirit with others. From the moment I was able to understand what true joy was, I wanted it, and I wanted to bring it to others on my path. I want to hold tightly on to internal blissfulness that comes from one joyful moment after another. I want to stay there in that meditative moment that tells me that everything is the way it is supposed to be.

Passions can embrace you if you hold steadfast to your dreams and goals in life. Joyful happenings are there at your fingertips when you work at becoming the person you need and want to be in life.

What are you passionate about? Begin to write down visions of what you embrace and dream about.

A single feather and its ability to move quickly in the blink of an eye can help you to embrace life as if every fleeting moment is full of spiritual happenings where there are angel sightings here on earth and in soulful times of insight and clarity.

Angel time

The thoughts of angels and other spiritual beings can bring you closer to empowering times. Can you remember the last time you truly did not care if someone believed you or not when you were speaking on spiritual topics?

Many people who are not spiritual are at a loss when serendipitous things occur; dismissing spiritual happenings as just a coincidence. I believe in spiritual interventions that I draw upon when in need of meaning and passion in life. I believe there are good people in our world. I embrace as fact that angels walk on the earth helping us to see with clarity what is good and whole.

I believe in magical happenings. I know that some things just happen and those good things propel and motivate us toward good and powerful self-exploration and self-empowerment.

Truth Time

The truth resides in you. You need to love yourself and love others; the most important goal you can complete in life is a love goal. Consider your many selves in the puzzle of life; bringing wholeness to living, and then bring it to others.

The most important factor in life is that you know how to love someone else with all of your heart and soul, only then will you be empowered.

Today, begin writing your love story.

Changing direction

Junctures in life bring on changes; some you ask for and some just are without choice. At every avenue in life you have a chance to change direction, and you should if you feel strongly about the need for change. Try different avenues and perspectives that make you feel happy and content inside. Be there for someone who needs you; that is the most loving and blissful thing you can do in life.

Mystery

Find special time for yourself in the mystery of life. You do not have to know everything that is about to happen on your journey. Allow things to unfold so that you are calm, unhurried in all that you do in life; thinking and planning before you plunge into a task, relationship or adventure. Concentrate on things that are important to you so that you see each detail in a colorful picture that is full of interesting color and forms of yellow, green and blues.

I walk every single day of my life, down the same path where I see things in newness every day. I do not miss anything. It is not the change of seasons that allow for differences in nature, it is how I look at it with depth; honoring all that my eyes can see. I would be lying if I said I do not fear change, but my goal is to find ways to allow changes to happen to me without feeling stress and anxiety over what evolves in my life, including relationships that may not be where I want them to be right now.

I strive to stop looking ahead too much at what is about to happen but rather I stay in every moment I have; relaxed with self-love and love for others. The only true pleasure in life is the joy I receive from caring for myself and others.

I believe in fantasy, fairytales with dragons and monsters because pretending is a good idea for reducing stress as do other modalities such as exercise and the soft ways of yoga; standing strong in *Warrior Pose*.

In fantasy land you can deal with life; knowing that the hero comes out of the fire after he or she fights off the dragons and monsters. It is a good dream where everything turns out with a *happily ever after.*

I know that life is not always a happy ending. It is full of ups and downs that challenge the soul. In the spirit of life where everything is internally yours I hope that you find that dreams are possible and some day you will fly like a bird. Believing in the impossible happenings of life is where we should all be with serendipitous happenings occurring often in the land of *Self-empowering feelings, thoughts and behaviors.*

6.

Become a positive story

If you are looking for ways to bring yourself to the positive side of life, read stories on how to be as optimistic as possible. Learn how to *just be in the moment* and mindfully get past any negativity there is in your life today. Allow positive moments to come into your life. You may have to work at it but it is worth the smile you will have on your face as you allow the negative moments to float by you again and again like a mindful experience that brings you to the present moment where you are happy and content.

Keep doing all the good you can

When you feel like things are not the way you would like them to be, keep on doing all the good you can for yourself and others. Good things will come to you when you are kind, caring and loving. The good times may not come as fast as you would like, but it will happen; there is always good and bad things in life. That is why you need to savor the present moment with internal stillness and whimsical, child-like wonder.

The water's edge

When some happiness comes your way, you will remember that you kept on doing those good things in life when it was difficult. Pause right now and think of a time in your life when you were happy. The scene may be the birth of your first child or a memory of childhood where you were content walking near the blue water's edge of a sandy beach where you stop and turn around; seeing your own footprints in the sand along with others who passed the same way you are going. Keep past good memories intact when you are troubled so that you can call on the vision of happiness in your life. When it is time, you will create or be given new happy moments because giving is the same as receiving.

Positive moments come to those who are seekers; whether it is in silence, reading an inspiring poem or it is with others who bring you comfort and love. You can have positive, loving moments, one right after another as you continue to be kind, loving and caring to yourself and others but you have to be aware that it is difficult but a meaningful and purposeful task each day to be optimistic.

It will not be easy continue on the *up side* of life. But the energy you create from internal optimism can be passed along to others as you move through the day, spreading a positive sprinkle of love on everyone you meet.

Walking down the street…

I saw 3 people on my way to a wake tonight, an older person had died so it was expected but he had so many friends that it seemed like a party instead of a gathering of mourners.

Of the three people I saw, the first was a man with a dog who was an older, plump person wearing a long white beard and struggling with a cane. It looked like he was blind because he tapped his cane back and forth, as his large brown and white dog looked up at him every so often; watching him and the sidewalk carefully for dips and cracks as they briskly walked in the cold fall night.

The next person I saw was a young man with dark, long and very straight hair with a slight built, and what I noticed was that he was in a hurry, walking as if someone may be following him; he wore a jacket that did not fit, and I wondered if he did not have many clothes to wear that were his own. Then I saw a woman who was much younger than me, maybe in her mid -forties. She had a striped blue and white shirt on with blue jeans and her dark brown hair was quite messy as she struggled to get into her car with a walker. My thought was that I had such a wonderful life; I should be the most positive person alive because I never struggled as much as these three people in their troubling moments walking down the street.

Autumn blooms in circles of beauty

The outside and inside of life: Secrets

It may appear on the outside that you are confident and in control of your inner self but on the inside, where are you? Do you trust your instincts on important matters that are happening to you right now? Or do you hide and have a place deep down in your soul where no one else can get in touch with you? If this is you, you have to come out someday soon and tell a friend how you are feeling and some of your deeper feelings; some sorrowful and some exciting and happy. When you are able talk about your secrets, you will find a release of tension and stress you may be hanging onto because you may be unable to *let things go.*

Finding liked minds

If you travel around looking to be with *on the surface* people who do not care about difficult topics such as exploring inner, soulful happenings, then you may not have to visit that dark or light place where no one enters and finds the *real you.* I have had experiences with both types of people; some who I know everything about and I would be surprised if they had any secrets I did not know and others who I have known for a long time and I feel strongly that I do not know them at all.

Where do the people in your life fit in?

Are you attracted to people who open up to you? *Open book souls* help your comfort level; making you feel uncomfortable at times but assisting you in becoming transparent and comfortable talking about feelings and taking first steps toward self-awareness, confidence and empowerment. As in the yin and yang of living there is a center with balance that is filled with loving and kind ways. Those centered and whole people are who I seek to help me along my journey in life.

Trusting and secrets

Some people have to feel they can trust you to keep secrets in order to tell you about their deepness; knowing that you will always hold their truths close to your heart. There are people who do gossip about others, and this may be their way to help themselves feel better about their personal, deep and silent ways.

What do you keep from yourself? Is your spirit trying to come out and become friends with you but you dust spirit off your shoulder like a fly has landed on you every time soulful waves of energy show up?

Now that I am older and closer to the truth about myself, I have found a new freedom that allows me to embrace others on spiritual topics. I provide assistance on growth and development topics in all avenues of mind, body and soul through my words of encouragement and how to develop a positive perspective. You may need a dose of renewed confidence in your personal spirituality which includes the ability to love all of your *many selves* including your spirit.

Being more positive than you want to be

Positive waves of pink energy move you toward calmness

It is easier to fall into the pit of negativity than to be positive, and there are people around who will not let you down; listening to your troubles. Wouldn't it be better to come out of the slump and be aware every time you are there in the midst of pessimistic thoughts so that you can stop yourself and carry on in a positive manner?

You can practice the skill of optimism. Being positive has a learning curve that may take time to develop, but it is attainable. I find that exercise is my best preventative medicine for a *slump* day. There is something about moving about and not thinking about anything except my next step that seems to energize me for the day, and the earlier I take a walk, the better my day becomes. If you believe it is too cold to walk outdoors, be aware that in the colder weather, you burn more calories.

Get out there and weather the storms for a dose of positive skill development.

Looking at other people's old treasures always makes me smile

You can help yourself become more positive if you include a hopeful attitude. Just about anything that you set out to do can be accomplished. Beginning steps of optimism may be as simple as reading an inspirational saying each day that helps you to focus on the good things in life.

There are wonderful happenings in the present moment. If you feel that there are more bad things right now, the good times do come along in life to spark your spirit into joy and gratitude.

Patient times

Be patient with yourself; practicing patience will allow you to see those little things in life that clarify the many reasons for rising from your slumber each day.

If you are older, cherish your wisdom; some of us do not get the honor

Where are you going on your path?

Today while sitting at a restaurant with an old friend we talked about how everyone in the restaurant looked older than usual. Of course it was the middle of the day when the children are at school, and any younger adults are at work.

The over 60 years

The diner was filled with older adults, no one under 60. Even the waitresses and cooks were all in their older years. Suddenly, I saw an old friend walk by in a very brisk way; arms swaying as his black, leather jacket moved with him, making creaking sounds. He was someone who had retired from the psychiatric center a few years ago; a Chinese minister for many years at the psychiatric center where we worked together. He did not stop to talk as he passed by, and I believe that he may not have remember me, or was in a hurry as he moved quickly by our table. We had begun our meal, and I did not pursue asking him if he remembered me.

Later on I had regrets not speaking with the minister because I thought about something he said to me while we walked through the Rose Garden, Delaware Park in Buffalo, New

York with some of our patients from the psychiatric center. He said with a broad smile on his radiant face, "You are the most inspirational person I have ever met." Afterwards, I thanked him and smiled.

I have thought for many years that it was odd for a minister to say I was the inspiring one when it was his passion as a person of spirit to be inspiring to others in their greatest time of need such as the pain and suffering of being hospitalized for difficulties of the mind and soul. His words will resonate with me for a lifetime because I believe that he was telling me to continue down the path of inspiring ways as he did. Today that is my continuing passion; creating waves of *spirit energy* to help others see that there is still time in your later years to have a meaningful life that you embrace with passion and love; passing this positive energy to others through kindness and compassion.

Doing the same things every day and seeing the same people becomes a blessing in later years

I love the comfort of sameness in my older years; it helps me to look forward to daily tasks, including some of the fun things I like to do such as painting a picture or writing a poem each day.

If you feel bored, add something challenges to your life. Beginning something that you never did before may *shake you up* enough to make your day full and happy. Think of things that would bring you pleasure; work again, volunteer for a cause that you are passionate about, find enjoyable people, and connect often.

Many people find creative things to do they just stumbled upon. Sameness can become the hobby that you develop on your own. Taking up new creative projects that you like to do every day can be exciting and just the thing to look forward to when you need to stay well in mind, body and soul.

Thinking back to good times

When I reminisce to times in my life that were good and solid, I visualize to a time when my children were young; running through the house laughing as the squeaky screen door slams and I follow them leaning out of the door saying,

"Don't stay too long on the beach, it is almost time for dinner, and they giggled, Okay mom, don't worry, we will be back soon."

Gifting

I am drawn to a special moment in life because it seems like it was yesterday, and as the days pass me by, I still focus on a vision of colorful red flowers sitting on my green and white hutch near my dining room window that I hand painted during artistic days of my life.

The flowers were beautiful, and sitting there for me when I walked into the dining room; a gift from my husband on Sweetest Day. That holiday, as corny as it is, meant something to me because I still remember saying to him, "Why did you give me flowers on Sweetest Day when you are going to leave soon?" Those pretty flowers marked the end of the marriage to me because it was the last gift my husband gave to me.

A tear rolls down my face as I think about sitting at the table looking at the gift of flowers. Today, I find that giving flowers is good way to honor a person you love. Many years have passed by since that moment, and I feel blessed that I have special moments in my life that I can still reminisce on when needed. Flowers, hugs from the kids and now grandkids are what I look forward to.

I am told that people change and forget to tell each other of their changes in life and that is why things end, but I know that everything in life ends; the good and the bad, and you are left to ponder on the good memories that bring a smile. Find your hugs, get close to someone, and do not struggle with anything in life. Allow things to flow with meaningful days, one after another.

Someday your spirit will rise strong above the clouds looking down, touching you with an energy that brings another positive moment in mind, body and spirit.

7
Ask for angel stories

I am feeling humbled inside as I look around at where and who I am. I have a blissful feeling inside my spiritual self where thankfulness resides because I am here to tell stories about angels on earth and up above.

I stay still here; in the internal hopefulness that I have about today being the best day of my life. I am here, able to stand strong with many branches of love that I stretch out to others with open arms.

Dee and Anne's angel encounters

Dig deep into your many soulful selves today and find some self-love, and share it with others.

"I remember a time when I thought I saw an angel, said Dee with excitement. "You must have seen something else," said Anne as she gently told Dee about how things really are in the spirit world. Anne seemed to know all about angels because she told everyone she knew that her time was limited in the mortal world. Dee was sure that angels who walked on earth were real because spiritual happenings seemed to happen to her when she needed it the most; finding comfort in a recent encounter where she felt like a special person who had recently passed to spirit was wrapped around her in a big hug.

In times of grief Dee needed strength and power to take her through some dark places in life that brought her light and joy again. Lightness is where good things happen;

flowers grow in deep blues, reds and yellows and the sun shines every single day, no matter what the weather because sunny places are inside the heart and soul of people who have angels by their side.

After Anne passed on to spirit Dee had many a spiritual happening with Anne's presence in many waves of energy and visions.

Angels are near

With angels near, you can feel the softness; embracing you throughout the present moment. A long time ago when Dee was young, for no reason at all she began to create angels, one after another. She said in a whispering voice to her mother, "Not sure why I am creating angels but I will give each angel I paint to someone who I believe may need an angel in their life." As Dee embraced this task painting angels, she asked her mom and aunt who were very religious why she was creating angels. They both told Dee the same thing, "Stay with creating angels because that is what you need to do; creating healing and love for you and others."

Dee knew that she felt better as she painted different angels, embracing spirit as she painted and the task of creating so many angels did feel so good that she went on for many months, stopping when a crisis came into her path. It was as if angels were helping her prepare for struggles in life where there is need for help.

A few months ago, Dee found one of her paintings that someone had left behind where she previously worked at a psychiatric center. She picked it up and remembered who she had given it to. A girl named Hope had needed help at the time Dee gave her the angel, but now is doing very well. "Perhaps Hope left the angel on the piano in a room where many people entered so that Dee would find it again." Dee is painting angels again but this time she knows why. "It is clear there are many people who need angels."

Angel Wings

Wings of angels are thought to be earned and as a soft bell chimes, another angel gets wings. Magical is the thought of divine angels flying above through the stars or gently sitting on a white, puffy cloud.

I believe that angels are here on earth, providing us with many positive moments and guiding ways to wellness. Angel interventions are many as I run into a few while walking down the green meadows of life. I have two special spirit angels; Anne and Angeline who are frequently by my side, providing me with guiding thoughts and inspiration. I see angels in nature, through the wings of butterflies and in reflections where I see spirit peeking through. As I walk through nature I find the changing colors, the smell of cinnamon along with the rustle of dry brown leaves in the slumber of a fall day, telling me that spirit is near me in yellow, red and orange ways.

The light in Dee

"Namaste" Dee said as she walked through the neighborhood to people she passed by. Saying hello is more with a Namaste which has greater meaning such as "the light in me sees the light in you." Today was different for Dee as she saw another Monarch butterfly. "For 3 days black and yellow butterflies swoop before me softly swaying as if to say, I am here and you need to see me." Dee felt spirit in the softness of a butterfly and she smiled as they passed in front of her, softly touching her shoulder. Dee's next encounter was a child and his grandmother.

Grandma had white short, fluffy hair and she carried her grandson's red book bag as she ran toward him saying in a loud voice, "Slow down or we will have to go home," and the boy carrying a large stick giggled and smiled as he continued to run ahead. The most joyful encounter on this daily walk was a wave and a moment for a talk with someone who made her day better and more enlightened to the magic of nature. It was the local minister; both had lived in a town called Wanakah for many years, Dee and the pastor had connected often on morning walks.

Sketch "Women Connected" is a tribute to the style of the Artist Gustav Klimt

Guided by Angels

There are angel guides everywhere in life. They are interwoven in our souls; giving a boost of energy that spreads through the glow of a single, pink flower. Angels hover nearby as I take a walk; singing and whispering loving words softly while I see bright, red birds often. Angels are inside of special people who ask if you need help with life. Angels are singing the soft music in our spirit that helps us to be guides to others.

Angels on earth and in spirit

There are reasons for everything that happens in life, good and bad. As a mortal being, I do not know what the reasons are. I am hopeful that when my spirt time comes, I will see with clarity all the many happenings I do not understand.

In this confusing world I try my best to *interpret* in my mind the reasons for different happenings in life. I believe in spiritual ways with my heart and soul that there is much more to learn as I become closer to my own spiritual awakening.

A person called Angel

I assume Angel was born angelic because they called her Angel. I am presuming this of course and that is why learning about the story of Angel is a wonderful experience to pass along to others.

Spirit beings do walk the earth and I know it because I have known and loved Angel all of my life and still envision her in spirit. Spirit beings are there for everyone, and their own human life may not have been the best but they made everything shine no matter what was happening.

They flourished under any circumstances; standing strong, centered and loving like a great tree, wavering but never falling.

Angel walked through mortal life in a perfect circle for 80 years; coming back to that exact spot where she began her life as a helper to others in many ways. Angel was the strongest human being I know which means that she had to come back in spirit to help others who she may have missed loving, touching and caring for along the mortal way.

Those who knew Angel wanted to be by her side because of the obvious healing effect she had inside. Even a minor touch on the shoulder brought on a smile, therefore if you stood in her presence for any length of time, things changed into softness, with negativity gone from your internal being. This healing effect stayed within your being; bringing you closer to angelic ways where negativity did not stay. Internal calmness, balance and love ran through your fingertips whenever there was a need to become more like Angel.

You ask, "Why are there people like this who are able to send out healing energy to others just by their presence?" And I tell you once again, "There are reasons for everything in the world, we just do not know what they are."

Recent touches of Spirit

I was touched recently by a stranger who I spoke with for a powerful hour of balance. This touch brought me inner awareness through physical, emotional and spirit touches of energy and peace. Right now, in this moment I am sending this healing wave to you who are reading this.

May love and harmony given to me a few days ago simmer within your thoughts, feelings and spirit; bringing you some light that you will pass along. If you have had a recent loss, remember that love is everywhere. It is in the swaying trees, the crunchy fall leaves and inside of your heart.

Angels are everywhere, surrounding, touching, helping, even if we do not believe. Spirit lives in everyone, and it is time for you to realize that you need to keep in touch with this soulful part of you because you need a spiritual component in your life. Your inner soulful self can help you to grow stronger in mind, body and spirit. Spiritual care is important. Find an angel inside of you, or on your outer core, surrounding you with love and harmony. Meditate, sing and chant with your spiritual side. Feel and touch angels who surround you.

Walk Early in the Day

Take a spiritual walk early when you rise and watch your shadow to find your spirit. Shadows embrace the wonders of the unknown. They surround everything, circling around the sides of a swaying tree, or softly touching your cheek. They surround you as you walk, touching and moving you forward. It may be difficult to walk against the pushing feeling of nature. Spirit is always in the ruffling of the fall leaves as they move and scatter; making crunching sounds that catch your attention. They are trying to teach you about believing that nature is full of spiritual happenings.

Time

Find time to delve into how to be touched by your inner self. Your spirit is your angel surrounding you with love. Feel spirit giving you a big hug; surrounding you in the warmth of an autumn day where you reminisce back to childhood, jumping into a large pile of crunchy brown leaves you have gathered after raking the lawn. You gently fall into the large pile, deeply hidden where no one can find you as they call out your name. You are silent in the darkness of a spirit leaf; peeking through to see the light of day. When someone passes along to spirit, they look for a good soulful person to surround. Angels know who to be near. I hope that you will someday be surrounded by a new spirit arriving in heaven.

Moments

Sometimes I need more than a moment to find clarity to ready myself for the next journey; taking my soulful ways through the white and gray sky where there are spirit beings to visit. It is a beautiful place to be; back to memories I treasure in the backyard of my favorite home where I am sitting on my deck petting my black and white Border collie we call Jesse.

Peace of mind

That quiet space between mind and spirit is needed daily to help you stay in the center of mindfulness where everything arises without sound for a long moment. You may need more than a moment to clear it all; readying yourself for the next journey to spirit.

On Being Mindful

Mindfulness, a form of meditation helps in the growth of self- confidence and empowerment. In silence and breath of a slower speed, you allow everything to float by you; negativity and positive visions pass by with acceptance and gratitude as you let go of it all, in the moment of a slow, deep breath.

Mindful is my beautiful place; I do not have to think about the now of the moment such as what I may have to do today. I am back and forth to memories treasured; floating by and landing in the backyard of my home where I am sitting on my deck petting my dog. Everything is sunny and joyful in this world I treasure with my children playing hide and seek in the yard.

Calmness and stillness becomes my friend as I move toward a spiritual sense of myself that feels good and loving.

When you become still in meditation, see spirit through branches of life that you create with clarity. In the tiny cracks of light, the breezes cross over you and spirit embraces life in nature. Find your breath in the single tree you stand by; becoming a self-empowering wave of wellness that you created.

Creative moments

Creativity resides deep in your soul bringing purposeful and passionate ways to others on your path in life. Share an openness and connectedness with other women that you have learned from throughout your life.

When I reminisce on my friend Anne and mother Angeline who are in the spirit world now, I realize how their strength helped me to learn and practice self-empowering ways; strengthening myself into a powerful woman

Self-empowering journey

Early on I was a shy person, unable to prepare myself for allowing life to flow in a way that was beneficial. I needed many mentors, and they helped me to see clearly where I should proceed in life in order to accomplish my dreams. For my career, I wanted many different levels of advancement, and I received the chance to find my way through all I wanted to accomplish.

My first degree gave me the ability to write well, a degree in English Humanities where I discovered that I would like to teach. I did not teach right away but I went on to my next degree in Registered Nursing where I discovered that I wanted to work with people less fortunate than myself.

Today I am free to choose anything I want to do, and in many moments of creative writing, painting, walking, meeting with friends, I create pictures that become visions of light for me and others. I continue down the road, no specific road but a path I feel peaceful about walking through each day that I have left on this earth.

For over 20 years I worked with the mentally ill at a psychiatric center where I did some teaching to others on how to work with people who had difficulties in their mind and needed to become mentally well. I supervised a treatment area and taught others how to run groups and activities that benefitted the patients. Before I retired from the psychiatric center I decided that it was time to become a teacher, and I taught at a local college in Buffalo, New York. There I taught subjects such as introduction to pharmacology, medical terminology, and Introduction to Human Services in the medical assistant program for 6 years. Today, I teach Yoga and have accomplished another dream in artistic ways. I am an artist who sells her work to others in the form of abstract paintings and as a designer of a clothing line that features my artwork; another vision that came true for me in my life.

Without the mentoring I had along the way from teachers, my mom and dad, and artistic friends along the way I would not have been as self-empowered as I am; finding that I could do all that I wanted in life and leave the shyness behind me; becoming the confident and empowered woman that I am today.

Pages of life

Each page I write and chapter I create can change life as I know it.

Every day becomes a new adventure where perspective is the only guide to happiness and internal, blissful events that only I can create. Chapters with many pages become the memories left behind that I can simmer on when I need to reconnect with life as it was in childhood.

I remember times in life where I could have chosen differently but I would still have had a similar life that I would grow into because early on from about 10 years old, there was a common thread of artistic and creative happenings I continued to be involved in that would bring some internal peace and smiles to others who needed joy to surface in life.

My work is to bring about a positive light into another person's life, or show someone through words and pictures that they can be a positive person who does not look back too long at the negative times. I know that a spiritual path has brought me to an awakening that I wish I would have found sooner because I was not as optimistic about life back in youth when I felt pressure to be a grown up and follow a specific, traditional path. Today I am grateful; feeling completely connected to life and the wonders it brings.

Coping with life

My tools come into life in art, writing and physical adventures including hiking, walking meditatively in nature and staying in yoga poses. What tools do you have in *toolboxes of life* that guide you into wellness and healthy living?

In the many pages of life there will be times of healing. Remember that it takes time to heal from difficult circumstances and there is need to develop tools to get through to the other side where light resides and darkness opens into orange color as the sun finally comes into view. I have found that the more tools I have to choose from, the better my outcome is in the vastness of becoming complete.

Ending with a story…

I see a boy walking briskly in the park with bright yellow curls on top of his tiny head, and the bluest eyes I have ever seen. He tells his mommy he wants a balloon. He says with a gleaming smile, "Mommy, I want the yellow one, it is so bright and beautiful." As they walked away with the beautiful yellow balloon, I remembered a similar scene with my own children and husband. We decided to let a bright, red balloon filled with helium launch from our home. We tied a note securely so that if anyone did find our balloon, they would call.

As we stood there ready for the launching of the big, red balloon, I was sad and happy at the same time because I knew it was fun to have fantasies but the reality of it was that no one would call. My daughters, Krissy and Sasha were young with dreams and magical happenings popping in their heads at a moment's notice. My husband and I looked at each other with a tiny chuckle, knowing that as soon as the balloon was out of sight, "that would be the end of that." On that particular day, I thought that I knew things in life pretty well; the way of the world, the way things are, and a belief that sometimes magic does happen on occasion!

The balloon stayed intact and landed about 500 miles away in Canada. We did receive a call and a picture of Joy holding the balloon. Joy was like her name; joyful and magical with a broad smile on her face in the picture she sent of herself. I enjoy telling this story of magical happenings because we all need some miracles in life, even small ones such as a magical balloon that lands in just the right place.

You may or may not believe in miracles, magical happenings or that happiness is internal but you can create your own fun times in life that fill you day with magic. Go back to places where you feel *child-like* again. Remember who you are and know that when you release a red balloon, it will soar in the sky and land somewhere that brings peace, harmony and love to your life. "Namaste; the light in me sees the light in you,"

Dory